My name is ______________________.

Draw a picture of your favourite funny character from a story.

____

(character name)

____

(story title)

Review: Clockwise letters m, n, r, h, k, b, p, j

Trace then write.

m n r m n r

M N R M N R

Trace.

meerkats munching merrily

Trace.

numbat nibbling noisily

Trace.

rat riding rapidly

Handwriting: clockwise letters; body letters (m, n, r).
Grammar: plural noun (meerkats), singular nouns (numbat, rat); adverbs (merrily, noisily, rapidly); doing verbs; possessive apostrophe (sailor's) ; adjectives (pink, delight); prepositional phases (in the morning, in the night).
Punctuation: upper-case (capital) letter to start a sentence; full stop.

Spelling and vocabulary: missed, moped, moved, needed, neigh, nod, noticed, roll, rub; suffixes –ily, –ing, –ed (noisily, warning, nibbling, needed); rhyme (night/delight, warning/morning). The word *numbat* is based on the word *noombat* from the Noongar language.
Literary elements: alliteration; ancient rhyme (over 2000 years old) for weather forecasting.

Trace then write.

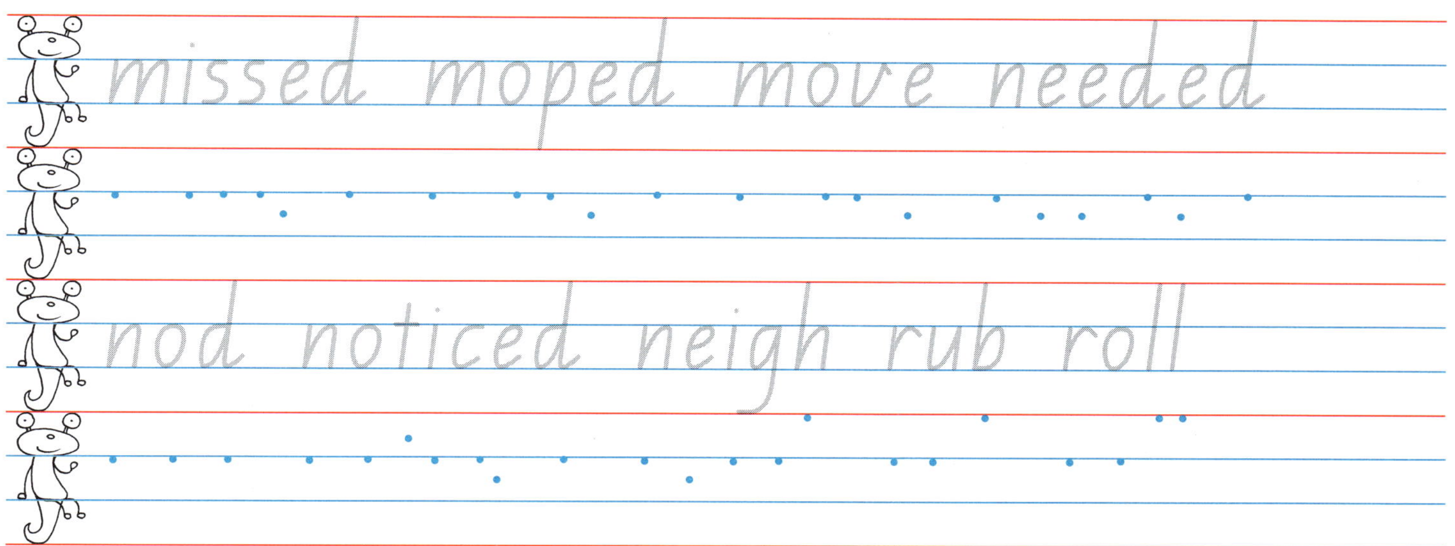

Trace then write.

Pink in the morning a sailor's warning. Pink in the night, a sailor's delight.

Self assessment

Draw a square around your best m.
Draw a circle around your best n.
Draw a triangle around your best r.

Review: Clockwise letters m, n, r, h, k, b, p, j

Handwriting: clockwise letters; head and body letters (ascenders) (h, k, b).
Grammar: singular nouns (hippo, kangaroo); adverbs (happily, kindly); doing verbs (bump, bury); question and answer; question word (why).
Punctuation: upper-case (capital) letter to start a sentence; question mark; full stop.
Spelling and vocabulary: beagle, bump, burped, buzzed, help, hippo, hit, hope, hug, kangaroo, kick, kneel; digraph 'ur' (burped). The word *kangaroo* is based on the word *gangurru* from the Guugu Yimithir language. The word *braak* is from the Gunai-Kurnai language. It means sulphur-crested cockatoo.
Literary elements: alliteration; riddle; joke; word play (died); onomatopoeia (burped, buzzed).

Trace and finish the pattern.

Trace then write.

help hit hope hug kneel kiss

kick buzzed burped bump

Trace then write.

Why did Bob bury his torch?

Because the battery died.

Draw a square around your best h.

Draw a circle around your best k.

Draw a triangle around your best b.

Review: Clockwise letters m, n, r, h, k, b, p, j

Trace then write.

p j p j p j
p j p j p j

Trace.

peacock prancing proudly

Trace.

jester juggling jauntily

Trace and finish the pattern.

Handwriting: clockwise letters; body and tail letters (descenders) (p, j).
Grammar: noun groups (a thousand miles, a single step); articles (The, a); adverbs (proudly, jauntily).
Punctuation: upper-case (capital) letter to start a sentence; full stop.
Spelling and vocabulary: jester, jiggle, jog, join, jostle, jump, peep, poked, pop, push, pout; digraph 'th' (thousand, with); 'le' ending (jiggle, jostle, single).
Literary elements: alliteration; Chinese proverb; onomatopoeia (pop).

Trace and finish the pattern.

Trace then write.

pout push poked peep pop

join jiggle jostle jump jog

Trace then write.

The journey of a thousand

miles starts with

a single step.

Self assessment

Draw a square around your best p.

Draw a circle around your best j.

Review: Straight-line letters i, t, l, x, z

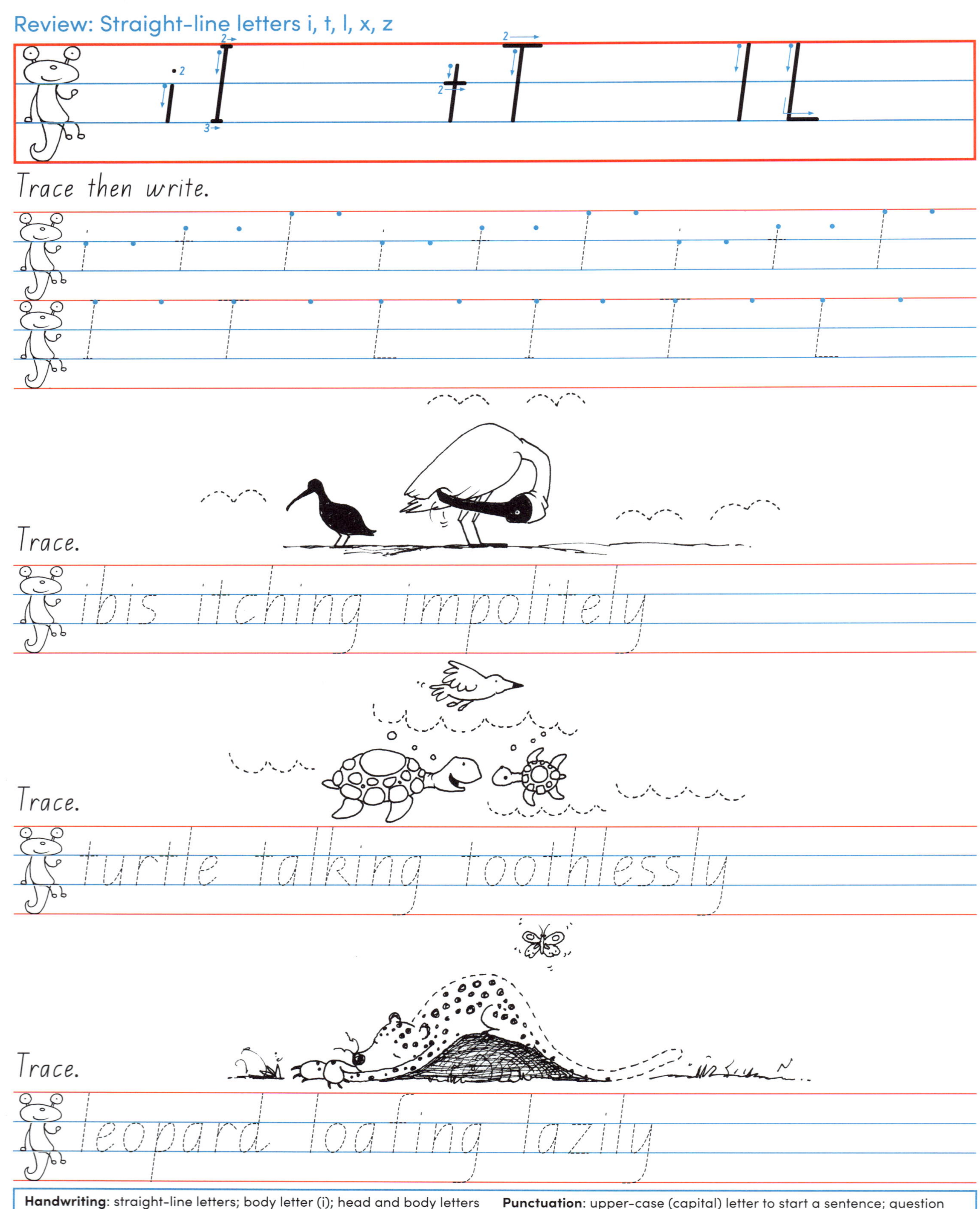

Handwriting: straight-line letters; body letter (i); head and body letters (ascenders) (t, l).
Grammar: prepositional phrases (on the ironing board); adverbs (impolitely, toothlessly, lazily); doing verbs (itching, loafing); saying verb (talking); being verb (are); question and answer; question word (why); adjectives (big, wrinkly).
Punctuation: upper-case (capital) letter to start a sentence; question mark; full stop.
Spelling and vocabulary: apostrophe for contraction (they're); changing y to add –ed or –ly (lazily, tried); homophones (to/too/two); leap, lift, lifting, loosen, lug, tell, trampled, tried, tripped, try.
Literary elements: alliteration; riddle; joke.

Trace then write.

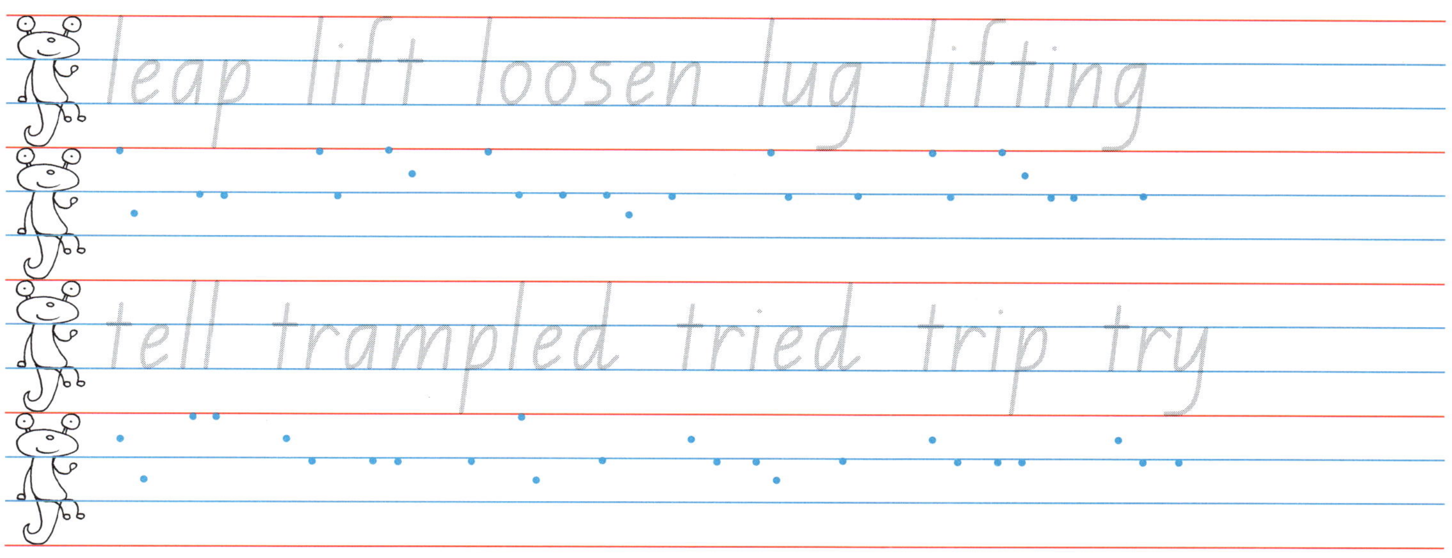

Trace then write.

Why are elephants so wrinkly?

They're too big to fit on the

ironing board.

Draw a square around your best i.

Draw a circle around your best t.

Draw a triangle around your best l.

Review: Straight-line letters i, t, l, x, z

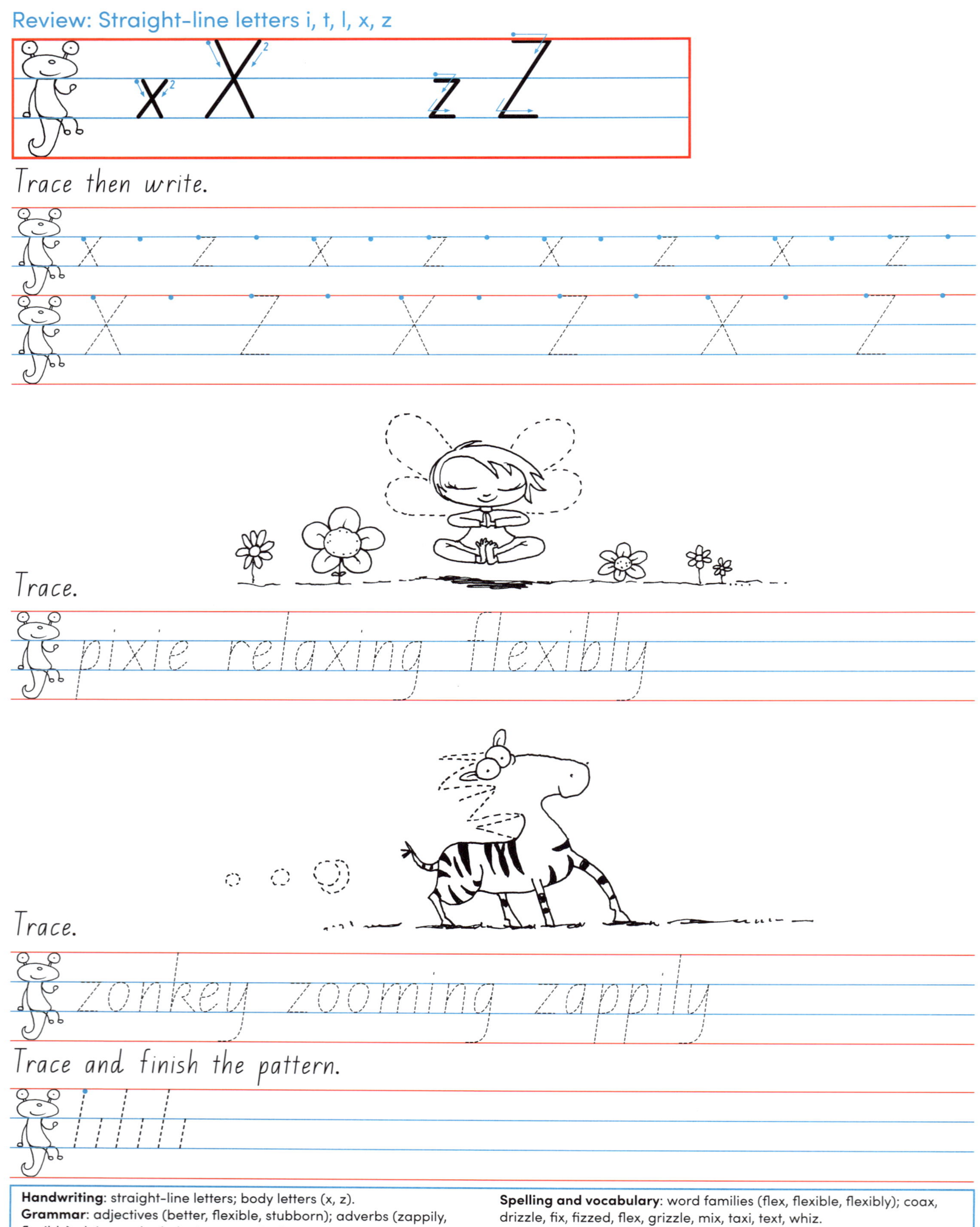

Handwriting: straight-line letters; body letters (x, z).
Grammar: adjectives (better, flexible, stubborn); adverbs (zappily, flexibly); doing verbs (relaxing, zooming); statement.
Punctuation: upper-case (capital) letter to start a sentence; full stop.

Spelling and vocabulary: word families (flex, flexible, flexibly); coax, drizzle, fix, fizzed, flex, grizzle, mix, taxi, text, whiz.
Literary elements: alliteration; onomatopoeia (grizzle, drizzle, fizzed, whiz); portmanteau word (zonkey = zebra + donkey); Aesop fable 'The Reed and the Olive Tree', moral: It is better to be flexible than stubborn.

Trace and finish the patterns.

Trace then write.

coax fix flex mix text taxi

drizzle grizzle fizzed whiz

Trace then write.

It is better to be flexible

than stubborn.

Self assessment

Draw a square around your best x.

Draw a circle around your best z.

Review: Anticlockwise letters u, v, w, a, d, q, o, e, c, f

u U v V w W

Trace then write.

u v w u v w

u v w u v w

Trace.

unicorn untying untidily

Trace.

vet viewing vocally

Trace.

wagun wobbling wildly

Handwriting: anticlockwise letters; body letters (u, v, w).
Grammar: personal pronouns (we); prefix and suffix (untidily); adverbs (untidily, vocally, wildly); doing verbs (untying, viewing, wobbling); statement.
Punctuation: upper-case (capital) letter to start a sentence; full stop.
Spelling and vocabulary: arrive, dive, drive, undid, undo, undone, unzip, upend, visit, vote, wanted, watched, waved, wished; prefix un- (undid); 'a' for short o sound (wanted, watched). The word *wagun* is from the Bundjalung language. It means brush turkey.
Literary elements: alliteration; Aesop fable 'The Four Oxen and the Lion', moral: United we stand, divided we fall.

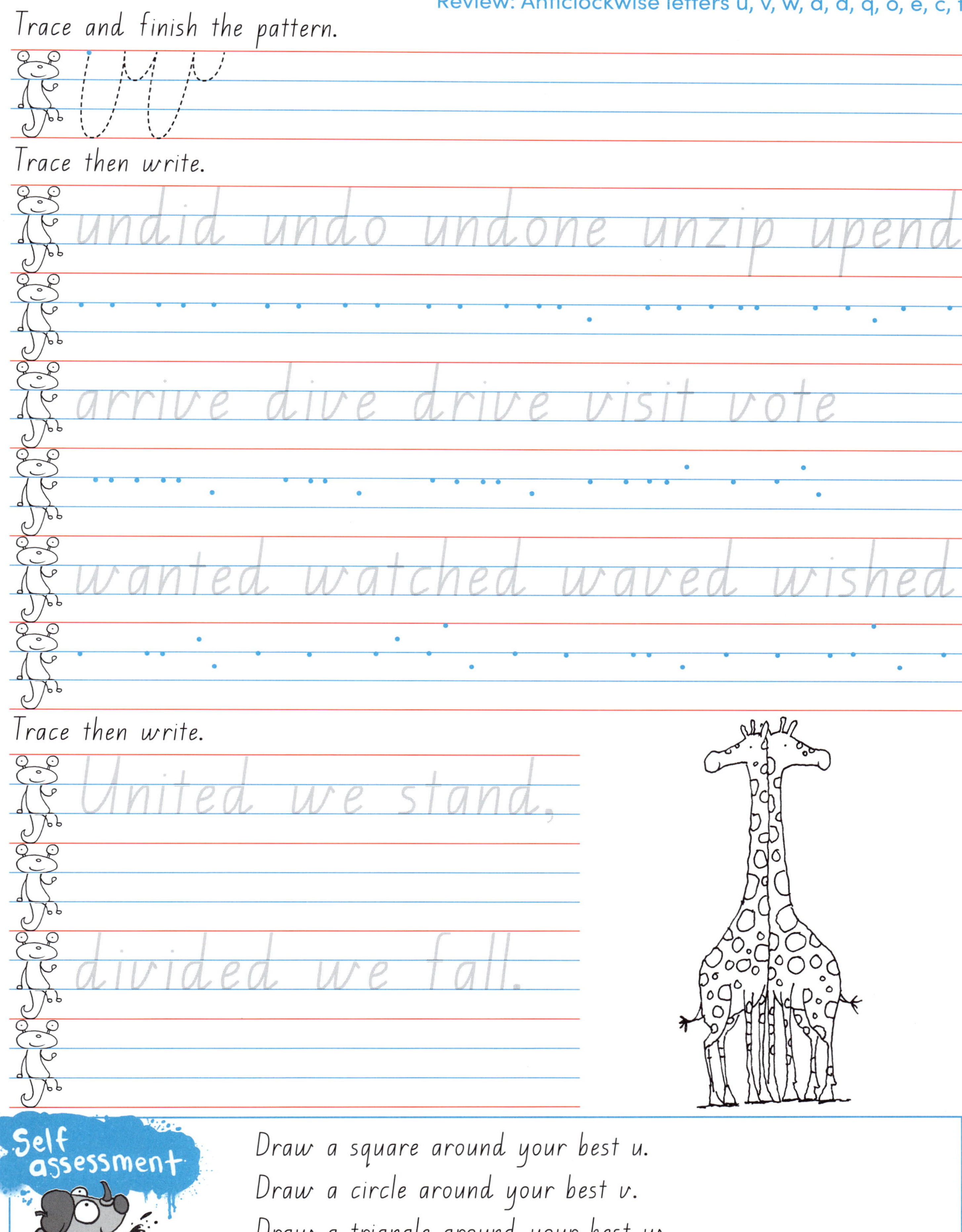

Trace and finish the pattern.

Trace then write.

undid undo undone unzip upend

arrive dive drive visit vote

wanted watched waved wished

Trace then write.

United we stand,

divided we fall.

Self assessment

Draw a square around your best u.

Draw a circle around your best v.

Draw a triangle around your best w.

Review: Anticlockwise letters u, v, w, a, d, q, o, e, c, f

a A d D q Q

Trace then write.

a d q a d q

A D Q A D Q

Trace.

ants arguing angrily

Trace.

dingo dancing daintily

Trace.

Queenie quacking quietly

Handwriting: anticlockwise letters; body letter (a); head and body letter (ascender) (d); body and tail letter (descender) (q).
Grammar: personal pronouns (I, you); adverbs (angrily, daintily, quietly); proper noun (Queenie); saying verb (quacking); verbs; question; question word (what).
Punctuation: upper-case (capital) letter to start a sentence; full stop; question mark.
Spelling and vocabulary: act, add, agree, drag, drop, droop; apostrophe for contraction (I've); qu and squ (quacking, squashed, squeezed, squished). The word *dingo* is based on the word *dingu* from the Dharug and Dharawal languages. It means wild dog.
Literary elements: alliteration; riddle; word play (quilt/cover).

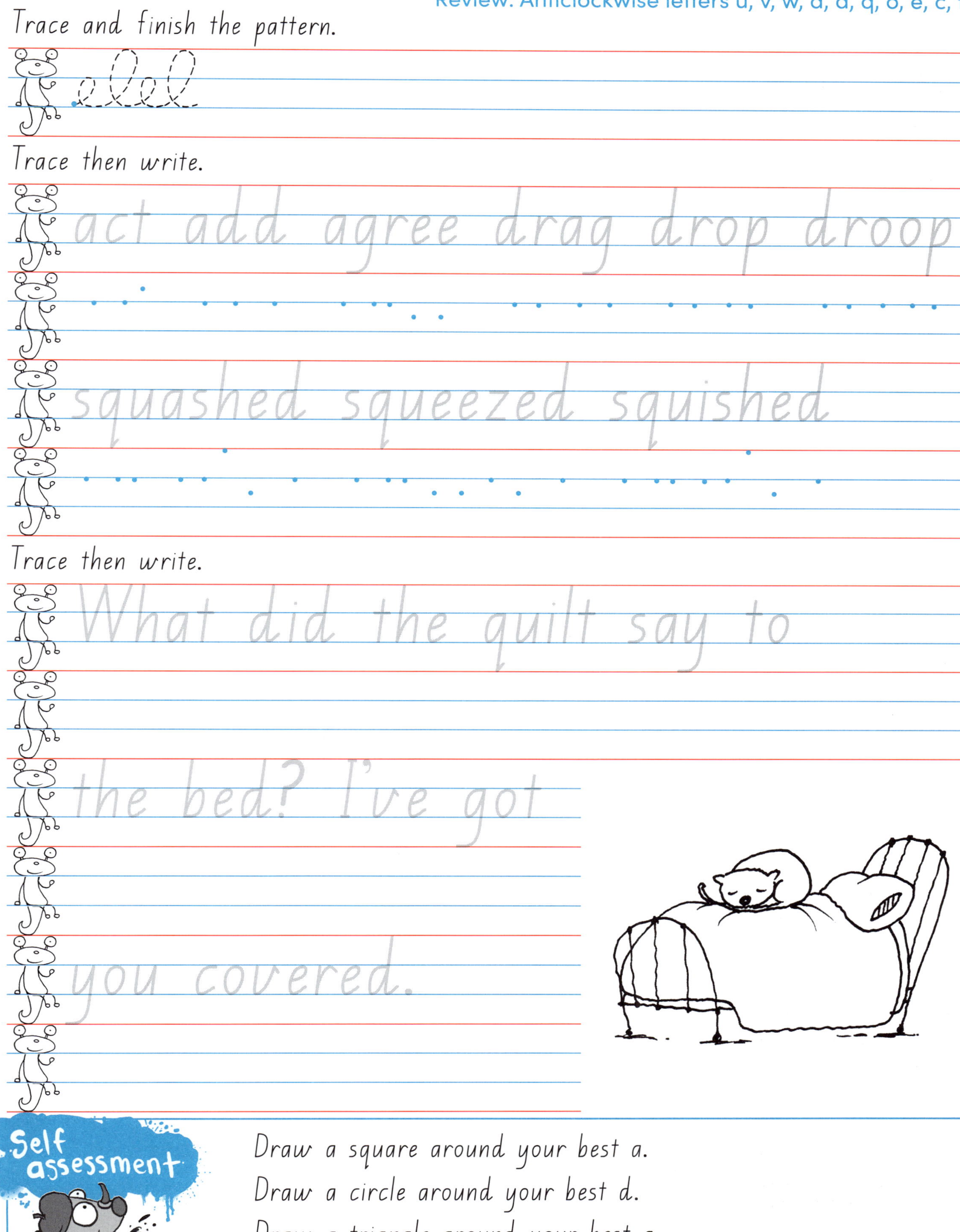

Trace and finish the pattern.

elel

Trace then write.

act add agree drag drop droop

squashed squeezed squished

Trace then write.

What did the quilt say to

the bed? I've got

you covered.

Self assessment

Draw a square around your best a.

Draw a circle around your best d.

Draw a triangle around your best q.

Review: Anticlockwise letters u, v, w, a, d, q, o, e, c, f

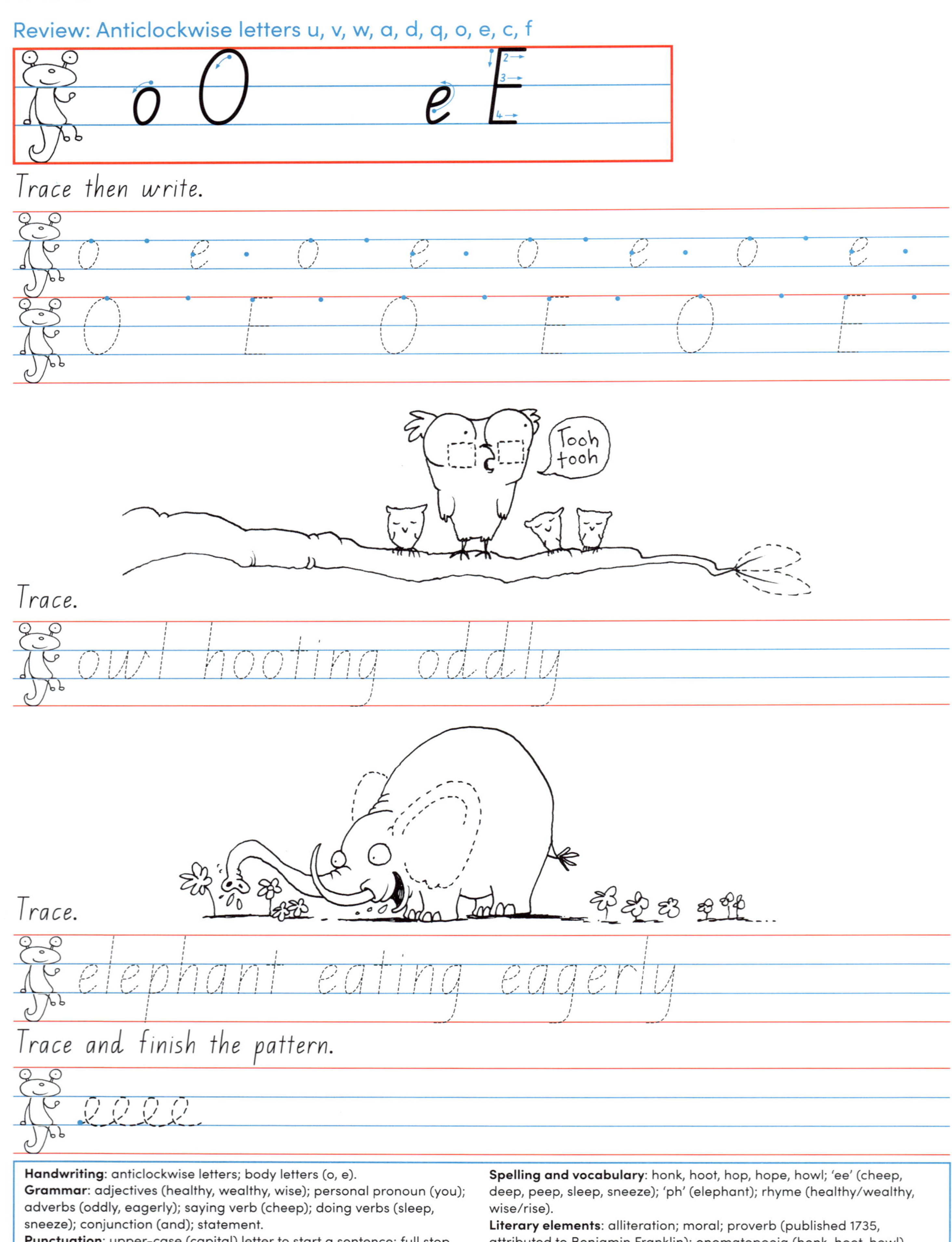

Handwriting: anticlockwise letters; body letters (o, e).
Grammar: adjectives (healthy, wealthy, wise); personal pronoun (you); adverbs (oddly, eagerly); saying verb (cheep); doing verbs (sleep, sneeze); conjunction (and); statement.
Punctuation: upper-case (capital) letter to start a sentence; full stop.
Spelling and vocabulary: honk, hoot, hop, hope, howl; 'ee' (cheep, deep, peep, sleep, sneeze); 'ph' (elephant); rhyme (healthy/wealthy, wise/rise).
Literary elements: alliteration; moral; proverb (published 1735, attributed to Benjamin Franklin); onomatopoeia (honk, hoot, howl).

Trace then write.

Trace then write.

Early to bed and early

to rise, makes you healthy,

wealthy and wise.

Self assessment

Draw a square around your best o.

Draw a circle around your best e.

Review: Anticlockwise letters u, v, w, a, d, q, o, e, c, f

Handwriting: anticlockwise letters; body letter (c); head and body letter (ascender) (f).
Grammar: adverbs (cleverly, freely); doing verbs (cutting, crept); saying verbs (croaked, called, say); being verb ('is' in where's); verb tense (creep/crept, fly/flew); question; question word (what); proper nouns (Mama, Baby, Pop).
Punctuation: upper-case (capital) letter to start a sentence; question mark.
Spelling and vocabulary: called, creep, crept, croak, croaked, flapped, flew, fling, flopped, fly; apostrophe for contraction (where's).
Literary elements: alliteration; riddle; joke; word play; onomatopoeia (croak).

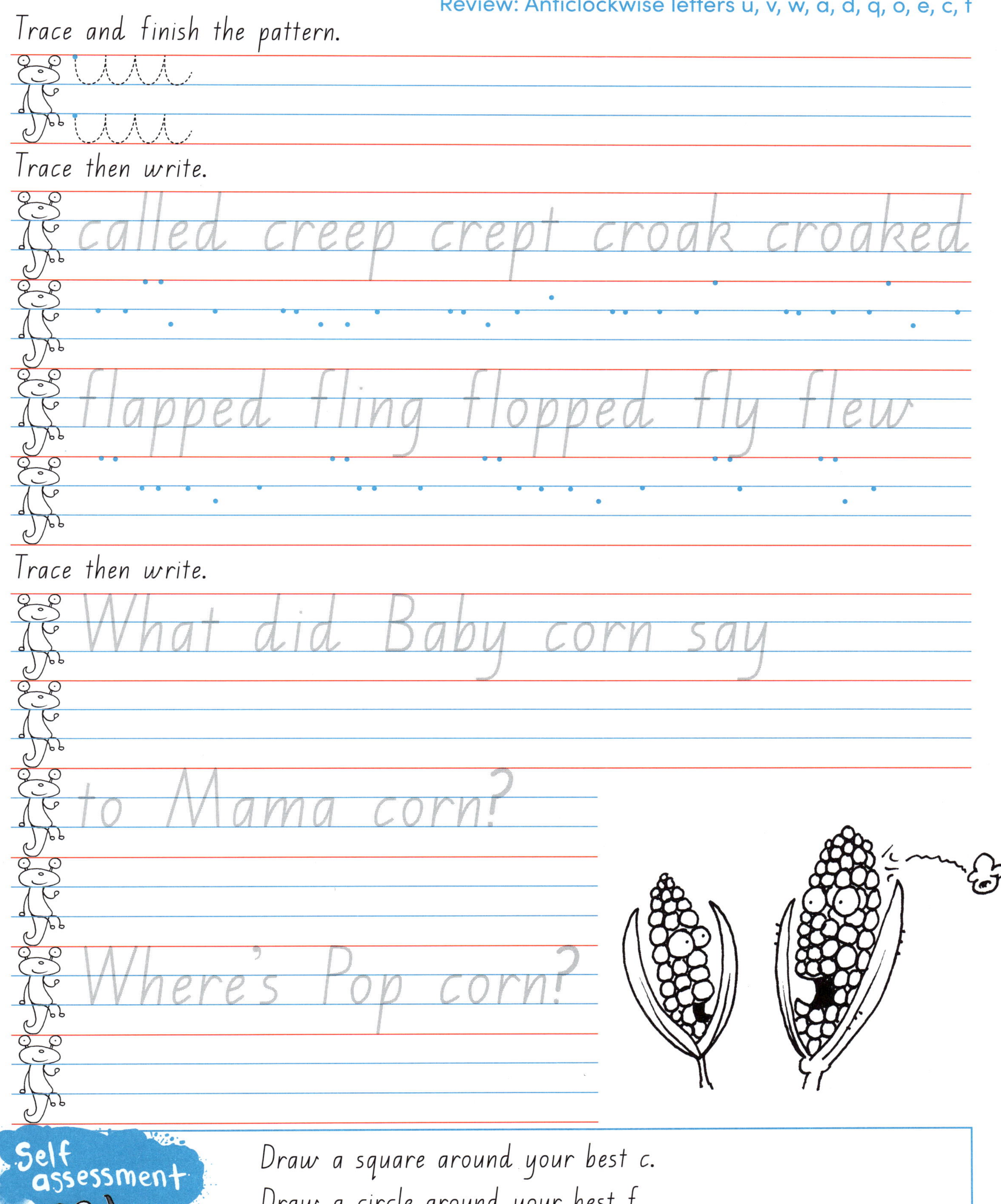

Trace and finish the pattern.

Trace then write.

called creep crept croak croaked

flapped fling flopped fly flew

Trace then write.

What did Baby corn say

to Mama corn?

Where's Pop corn?

Self assessment

Draw a square around your best c.

Draw a circle around your best f.

Review: Direction change letters g, y, s

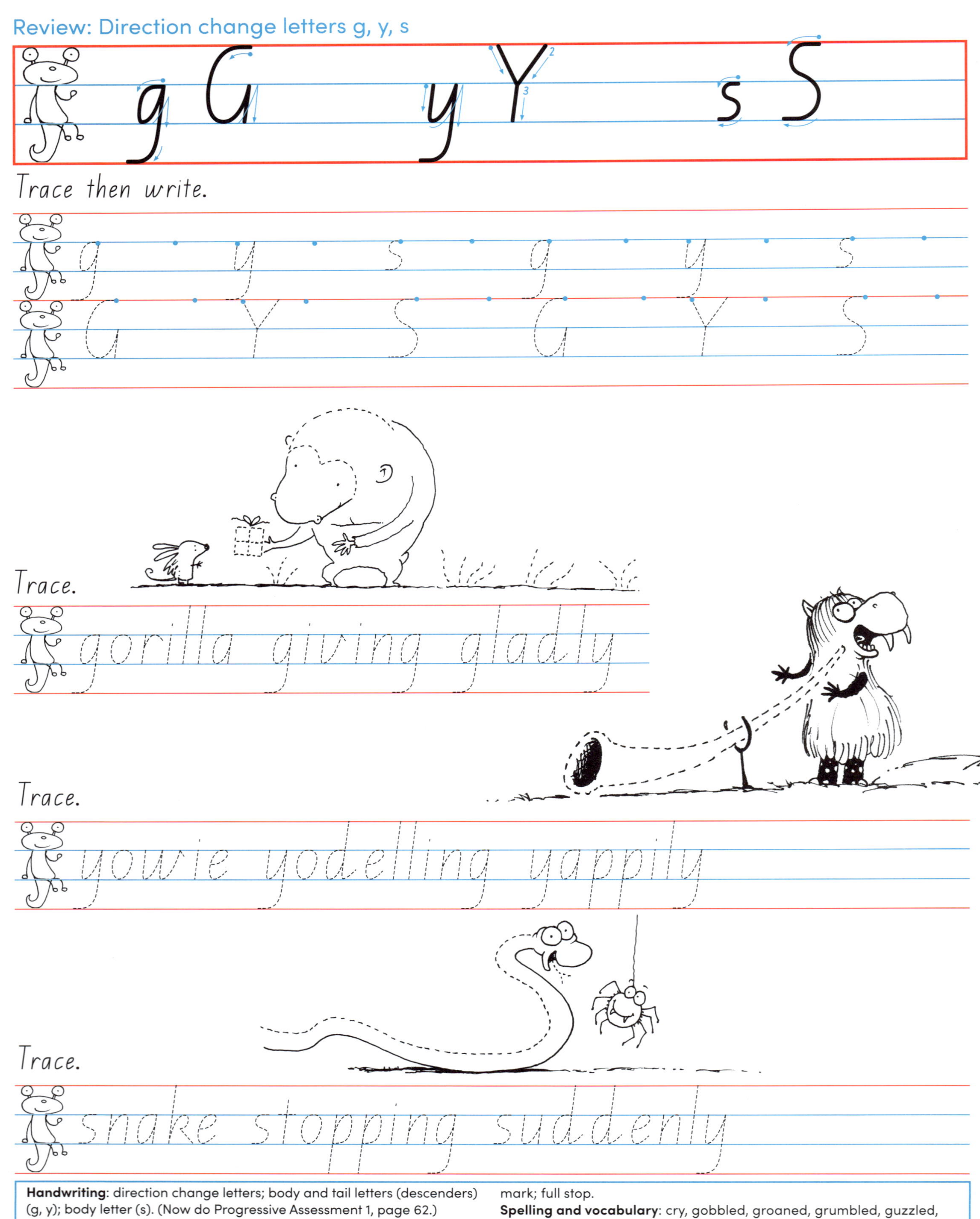

Handwriting: direction change letters; body and tail letters (descenders) (g, y); body letter (s). (Now do Progressive Assessment 1, page 62.)
Grammar: noun – pronoun reference (dragons-they); adverbs (gladly, yappily, suddenly); past tense (-ed); question; question word (why); saying verbs (grumbled, groaned, yodelling).
Punctuation: upper-case (capital) letter to start a sentence; question mark; full stop.
Spelling and vocabulary: cry, gobbled, groaned, grumbled, guzzled, say, sob, stop, swap, swing, try, yawn, yell, yelled; silent 'k' (knight). The word *yowie* is from the Yuwaalaraay language.
Literary elements: alliteration; riddle; joke; word play (knight/night); homophones (knight/night).

Trace then write.

gobbled groaned grumbled

cry try yawn yell yelled

say sob stop swap swing

Trace then write.

Why do dragons sleep all day?

So they can go fight knights.

Draw a square around your best g.
Draw a circle around your best y.
Draw a triangle around your best s.

Review: Numerals

Trace then write.

0 1 2

3 4 5 6 7

8 9 10 11 12

13 14 15 16

17 18 19 20

There are 7 days in a week

and 12 months in a year.

Trace.

There are 365 days in a year

and 366 days in a leap year.

Draw a star around your best numeral.

Draw a triangle around a numeral you could improve.

Trace then write.

30 days has

September, April, June and

November. All the rest

have 31 except February,

which has 28 days clear

and 29 each leap year.

Draw a frame around each numeral.

Tick the numeral with the highest value.

How many words name months of the year?

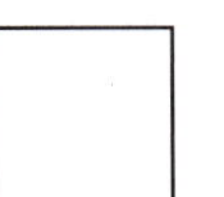

Trace then write.

10 ten 20 twenty 30 thirty

40 forty 50 fifty 60 sixty

70 seventy 80 eighty 90 ninety

100 one hundred

1st first 2nd second 3rd third

Circle and label your BEST handwriting on this page as 1st, 2nd or 3rd.

Trace then write in correct NUMBER order.

fifty sixty forty

Trace then link the numeral to the number word.

thirty 8 eighty 9 90 seventy

70 nine 80 eight 30 ninety

Trace then write in correct ALPHABETICAL order.

twelve fifteen eleven

Trace then write in correct ALPHABETICAL order.

twenty eighteen nineteen thirteen

Trace then write in correct ALPHABETICAL order.

fourteen twelve seventeen ten

Draw a box around your neatest handwritten word.

Draw a circle around your best handwritten numeral.

Look! c, e and d already have exits.

c e d

Trace.

c c c c c e e e e e d d d d d

a → a → a

Write the letter . . . then quickly change direction . . . to make an exit.

Track.

Handwriting: exits from a, c, d, e, h, k, l, t.
Grammar: adverb (away); articles (an, a, the); statement.
Punctuation: upper-case (capital) letter to start a sentence; full stop.
Spelling and vocabulary: rhyme (away/day).
Literary elements: Welsh proverb (Eat an apple on going to bed and you'll keep the doctor from earning his bread).

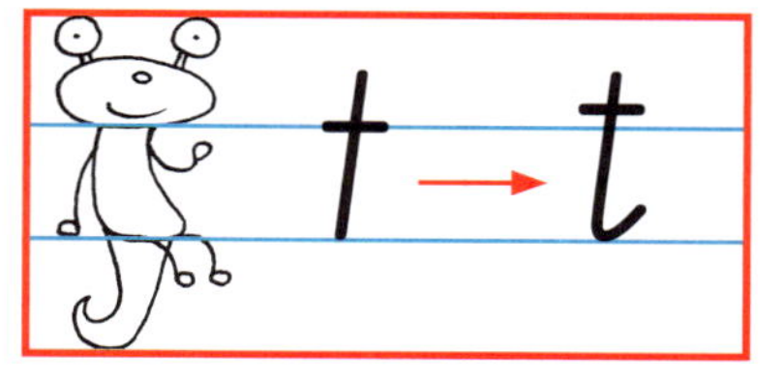

When you add an exit to t, lift the crossbar above the line.

Track.

  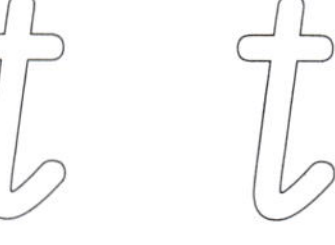       

Trace then write.

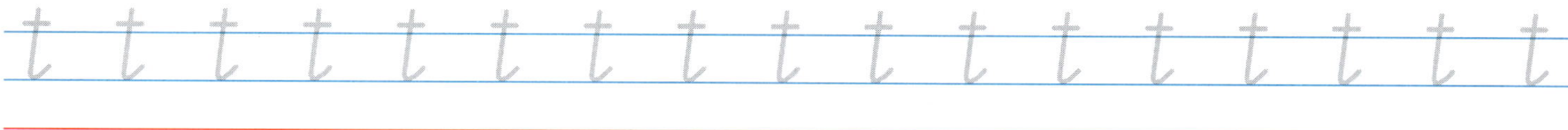

a c d e h k l t h k a c d e l

Trace then write.

doctor away.

Draw a square around your best letter with an exit.
Underline any letters you could improve.

Exits: a, c, d, e, h, k, l, t

Trace.

Write words of your own using the letters above. Remember to add exits.

Handwriting: exits from a, c, d, e, h, k, l, t.
Grammar: question; question word (when); noun – pronoun reference (dinosaurs-they); plural nouns; personal pronoun (they); statement.
Punctuation: upper-case (capital) letter to start a sentence; question mark; full stop.
Literary elements: riddle; joke; word play (dinosaur/sore).

Write.

a

h

k

l

t

Trace then write.

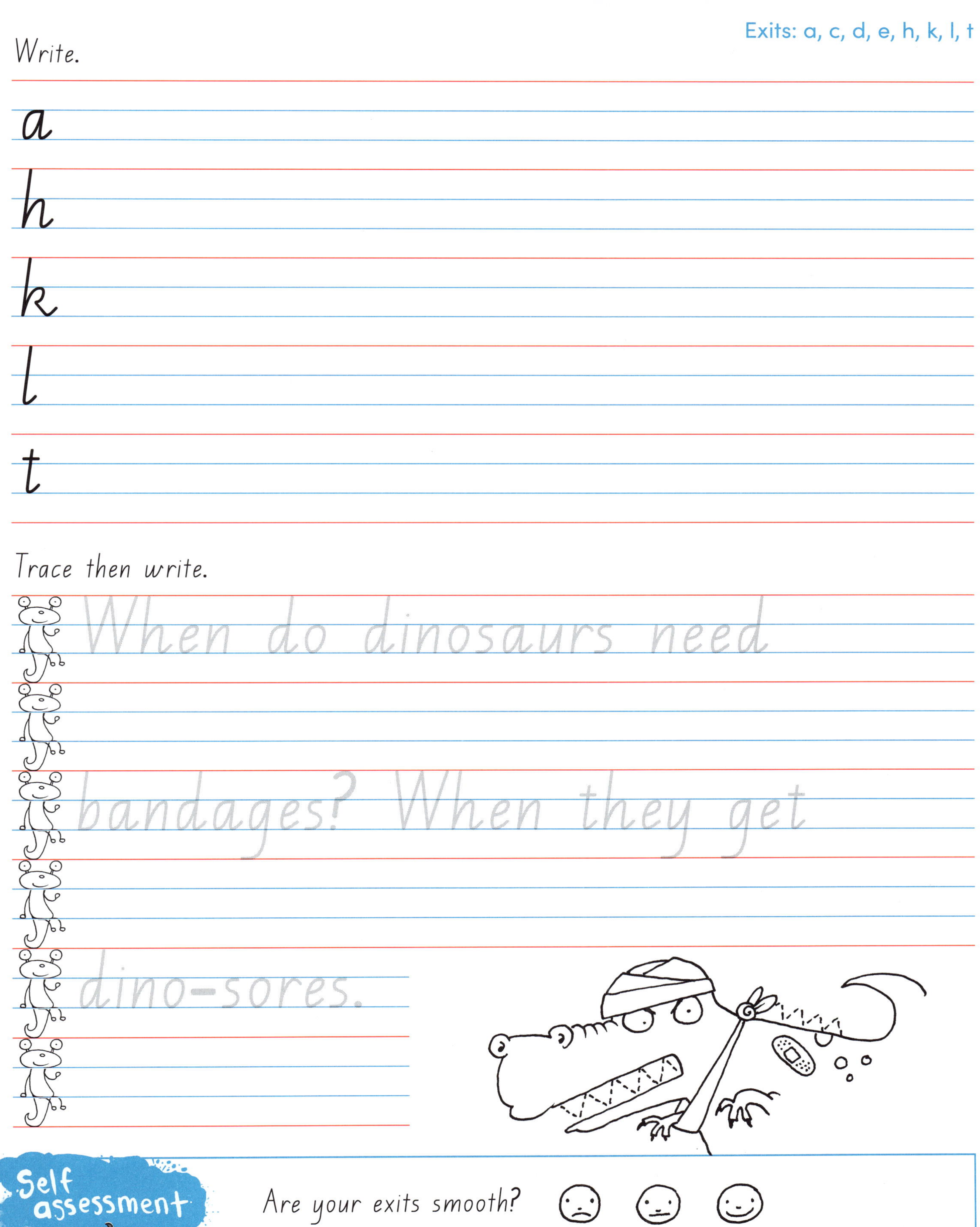

When do dinosaurs need bandages? When they get dino-sores.

Self assessment

Are your exits smooth?

Exits: a, c, d, e, h, k, l, t

Find and trace the letters that have exits.

a g d c s t l o e r

Trace and add exits.

a c d e h k l t

Use th to start these words. Trace the words.

_ _ e _ _ is _ _ at _ _ en

_ _ ey _ _ em _ _ eir _ _ ere

_ _ ree _ _ ank _ _ rough

_ _ rew _ _ row _ _ ink

Use ed or de to complete each word.

ro _ _ ri _ _ fri _ _ si _ _

ma _ _ tri _ _ tir _ _ hi _ _

gli _ _ cri _ _ spi _ _ sli _ _

Handwriting: exits from a, c, d, e, h, k, l, t.
Grammar: being verbs (aren't, are); noun – pronoun reference (leopards–they).
Punctuation: upper-case (capital) letter to start a sentence; question mark; full stop.
Spelling and vocabulary: apostrophe for contraction (aren't); words ending in –ed or –de; digraph 'th'.
Literary elements: riddle; word play (spotted).

Trace then write the matching lower case letters.

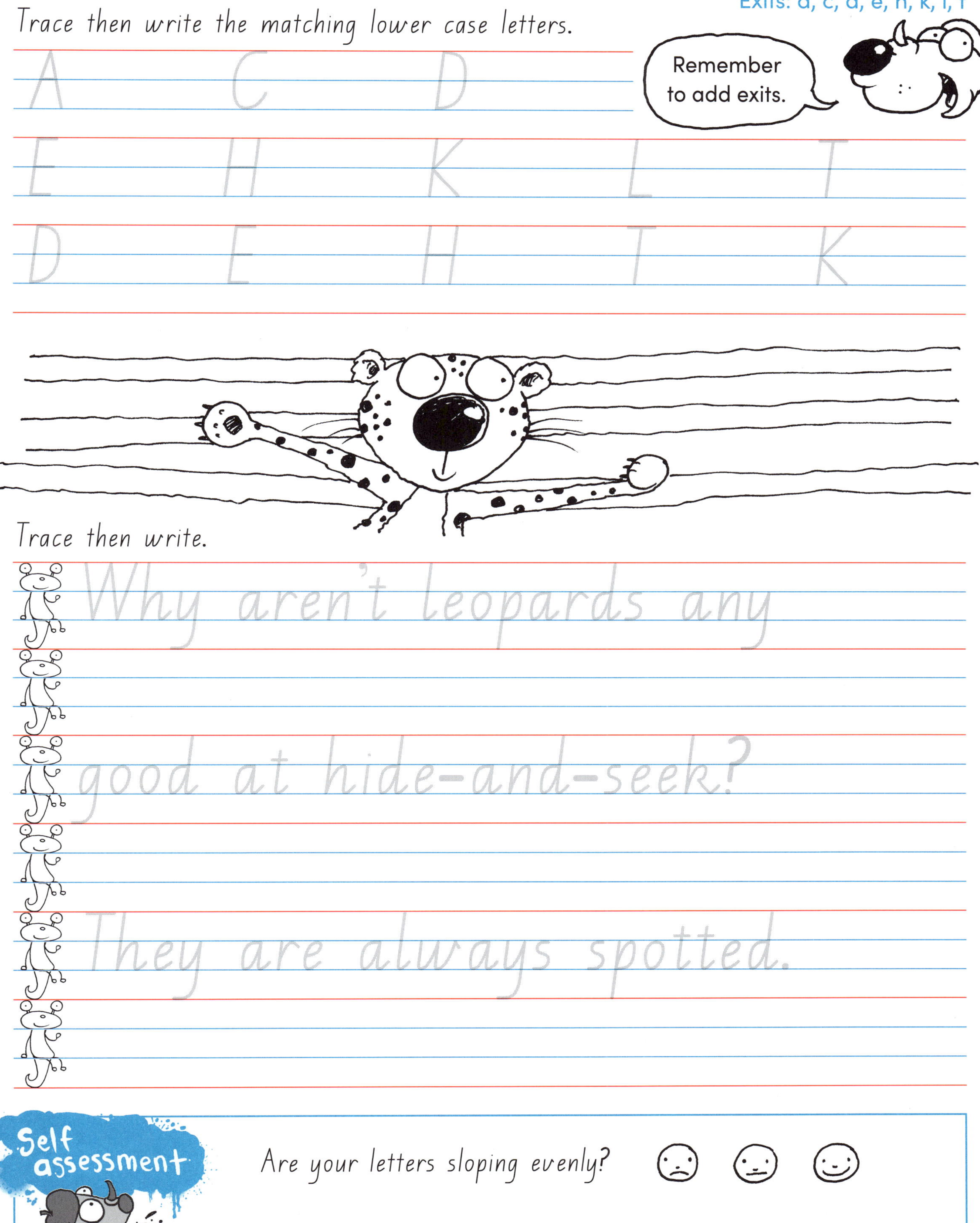

Trace then write.

Self assessment

Are your letters sloping evenly?

Exits: a, c, d, e, h, k, l, t

Use ch to start these words. Trace the words.

__ icken __ op __ omp __ ase

__ oose __ ose __ in __ ange

Use ce to complete each word.

poli __ mi __ flee __ li __

pea __ pie __ ni __ di __

Use lk or ck to complete each word.

li __ si __ chi __ fli __

wa __ ta __ cha __ sta __

ki __ ti __ sti __ pi __

Handwriting: exits from a, c, d, e, h, k, l, t. (Now do Progressive Assessment 2, page 62.)
Grammar: prepositional phrase (in the pocket); being verb (is); doing verb (carried)
Punctuation: upper-case (capital) letter to start a sentence; question mark; full stop.
Spelling and vocabulary: words ending in 'lk'; digraphs 'ch', 'ck'; silent e (ce); homophones (peace/piece).
Literary elements: joke; riddle; word play (ticks, face); simile (like a garden); Chinese proverb.

Trace then write.

Who has a face

two hands and

ticks? A teacher.

Trace then write.

A book is like a garden

carried in the pocket.

Self assessment

My exits are smooth and neat:

sometimes ☐ often ☐ always ☐.

When you start to join letters, an **entry** will help you get from one letter to the next. These letters have round entries: r, m, n, x.

Curve up . . . then write the letter.

Track.

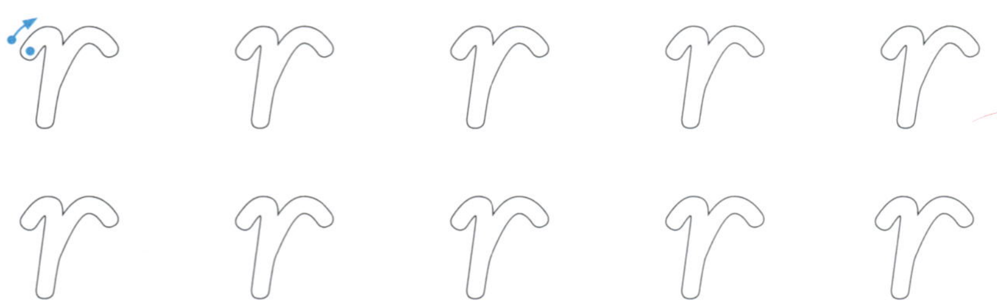

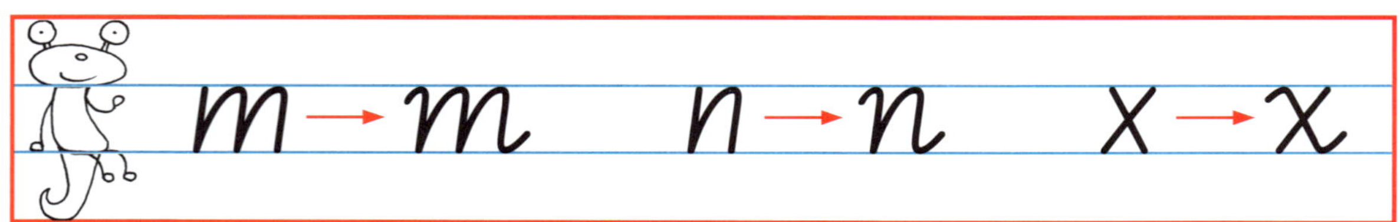

Track.

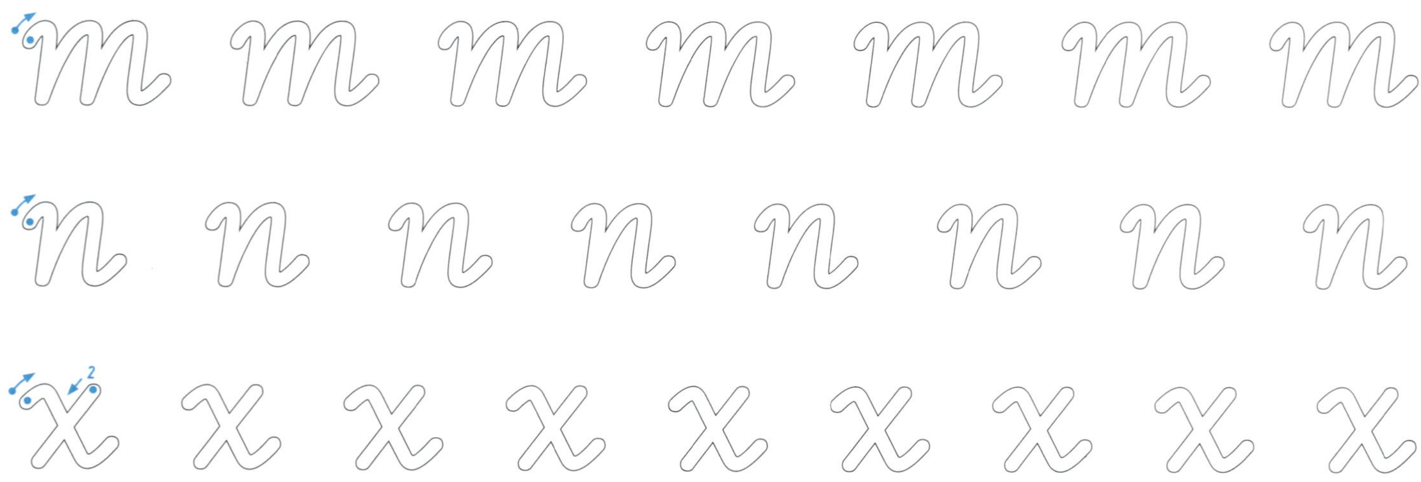

Handwriting: rounded entries to r, m, n, x.
Grammar: question; question word (why); being verb (are); saying verb (called); statement.
Punctuation: upper-case (capital) letter to start a sentence; question mark; exclamation mark; upper-case (capital) for loud exclamation.
Literary elements: riddle; word play (are/aRRR); onomatopoeia (aRRR).

Trace.

r r r r r r r r r r r r r r r

m m m m m m m m m m m

n n n n n n n n n n n n n

x x x x x x x x x x x x x x

r m n x r n m x r n m x

Trace then write.

Why are pirates called

pirates? Because they aRRR!

Self assessment

My posture is comfortable:

sometimes ☐ often ☐ always ☐.

Rounded entries: r, m, n, x

Trace then write.

m n m n m n m n m n m n

r x r x r x r x r x r x

Use x to complete each word. Trace the words.

ne_t e_it te_t fle_

a_e fi_ fo_ fla_ mi_

Remember the entries and exits.

Use an to complete each word. Trace the words.

__t __gle __telope d__ce

t__gle wr__gle str__gle

Trace then write the matching lower-case letters.

R M N X

ENTRY

Handwriting: rounded entries to r, m, n, x. (Now do Progressive Assessment 3, page 63.)
Grammar: question; question word (what); proper nouns (Mars, Martian); adjectives (soft, white); conjunction (and); prepositional phrase (on Mars); being verb ('is' in What's).
Punctuation: upper-case (capital) letter to start a sentence; question mark.
Spelling and vocabulary: apostrophe for contraction (What's); rhyme (dangle/strangle); words ending in 'le'.
Literary elements: riddle; word play (Martian-mallow/marshmallow).

Use ma or ra to complete the words. Trace the words.

__in __ng __ne __nch

d__g __ngle __ny __te

__id sc__tch __tch

__ybe d__in d__gon

Trace then write.

What's soft and white

and lives on Mars?

A Martian-mallow.

Are your rounded entries smooth?   

i, j, p, u, v, w
and y have
pointed entries.
For these letters, make sure your
entries are sharp not round.
Make a short
straight line . . .
then write the letter.
Track.
Look!
i and u have
pointed entries
but rounded
exits.
Track.

Track.
Remember to make your pointed entries sharp.
Trace then write.
Self assessment
Are your pointed entries sharp?

Pointed entries: i, j, p, u, v, w, y

Trace then write.

u u u u u u u u u u u u u

v v v v v v v v v v v v v

w w w w w w w w w w w

y y y y y y y y y y y y y y

Write.

i j

p u

v w

y

Handwriting: pointed entries to i, j, p, u, v, w, y.
Grammar: question; question words (what, why); proper noun (Wendy); noun group (her watch); prepositional phrases (under an umbrella, out the window)
Punctuation: upper-case (capital) letter to start a sentence; question mark; full stop.
Spelling and vocabulary: 'ow' (window, throw); 'a' for short 'o' sound (watch, wanted).
Literary elements: riddle; homonym word play (wrist watch/watch time fly); homophone word play (rein/rain).

Trace then write.

Pointed entries: i, j, p, u, v, w, y

What animal needs to stand

under an umbrella?

A reindeer.

Trace then write.

Why did Wendy throw

her watch out the window?

To see time fly.

Self assessment

Which letter did you find easiest to give a pointed entry?

Use y to complete each word. Trace the words.

pupp_ bo_ to_ fl_ librar_

part_ pon_ gupp_ bunn_

stingra_ bab_ monke_

Use y or ie to complete each word. Trace the words.

pupp_ _s bo_s to_s fl_ _s

librar_ _s part_ _s pon_ _s

gupp_ _s bunn_ _s stingra_s

bab_ _s monke_s

Handwriting: pointed entries to i, j, p, u, v, w, y.
Grammar: question; question word (where); personal pronouns (you); prepositional phrases (In the barking lot).
Punctuation: upper-case (capital) letter to start a sentence; question mark.
Spelling and vocabulary: words ending in 'y'; changing 'y' to 'i' to add 'es' for plurals (puppy/puppies); rhyme (guppy/puppy).
Literary elements: riddle; word play (barking/parking).

Trace and add entries and exits to the letters.

i j p r n m x a d

c e h k l u w v y

Trace then write the matching lower case letters.

I J P U J

V W Y W Y

Trace then write.

Where can you leave

your dog while you shop?

In the barking lot.

Self assessment

Draw a tick over each letter in the riddle that has a pointed entry. How many did you find?

Use ing to complete each word. Write the word.

play_ _ _ help_ _ _ runn_ _ _

jump_ _ _ work_ _ _ pull_ _ _

draw_ _ _ shiver_ _ _

Remember! u has a pointed entry, but n has a rounded entry.

Use un to complete each word. Write the word.

_ _do _ _wrap _ _afraid

_ _beatable _ _even _ _happy

Handwriting: pointed entries to i, j, p, u, v, w, y. (Now do Progressive Assessment 4, page 63.)
Grammar: question; question word (what) ; personal pronoun (you, it).
Punctuation: upper-case (capital) letter to start a sentence; question mark.
Spelling and vocabulary: suffix –ing; prefix un–; compound words with 'up'.
Literary elements: riddle; word play (tooth hurty/two thirty).

Trace then write.

uphill upstairs upwards upset

upfront upon uplifting upkeep

Trace then write.

What time is it when you

go to the dentist?

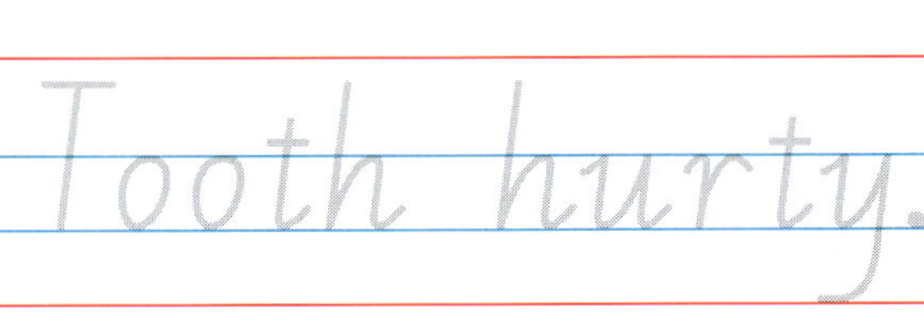

Tooth hurty.

Draw a circle around your neatest word.

Draw a square around a word you could improve.

Letters that change: f

Handwriting: letters that change (f).
Grammar: question; question word (what); proper nouns (Frank, Friday); adjectives (stuffy, fluffy) ; saying verb (said); personal pronoun ('I' in I'll); suffixes (fluff-fluffy); nouns that don't change their form for plurals (fish).
Punctuation: quotation marks; upper-case (capital) letter to start a sentence; question mark; statement; full stop.
Spelling and vocabulary: rhyme (huff/puff).
Literary elements: reference to folktale *The Three Little Pigs*; riddle.

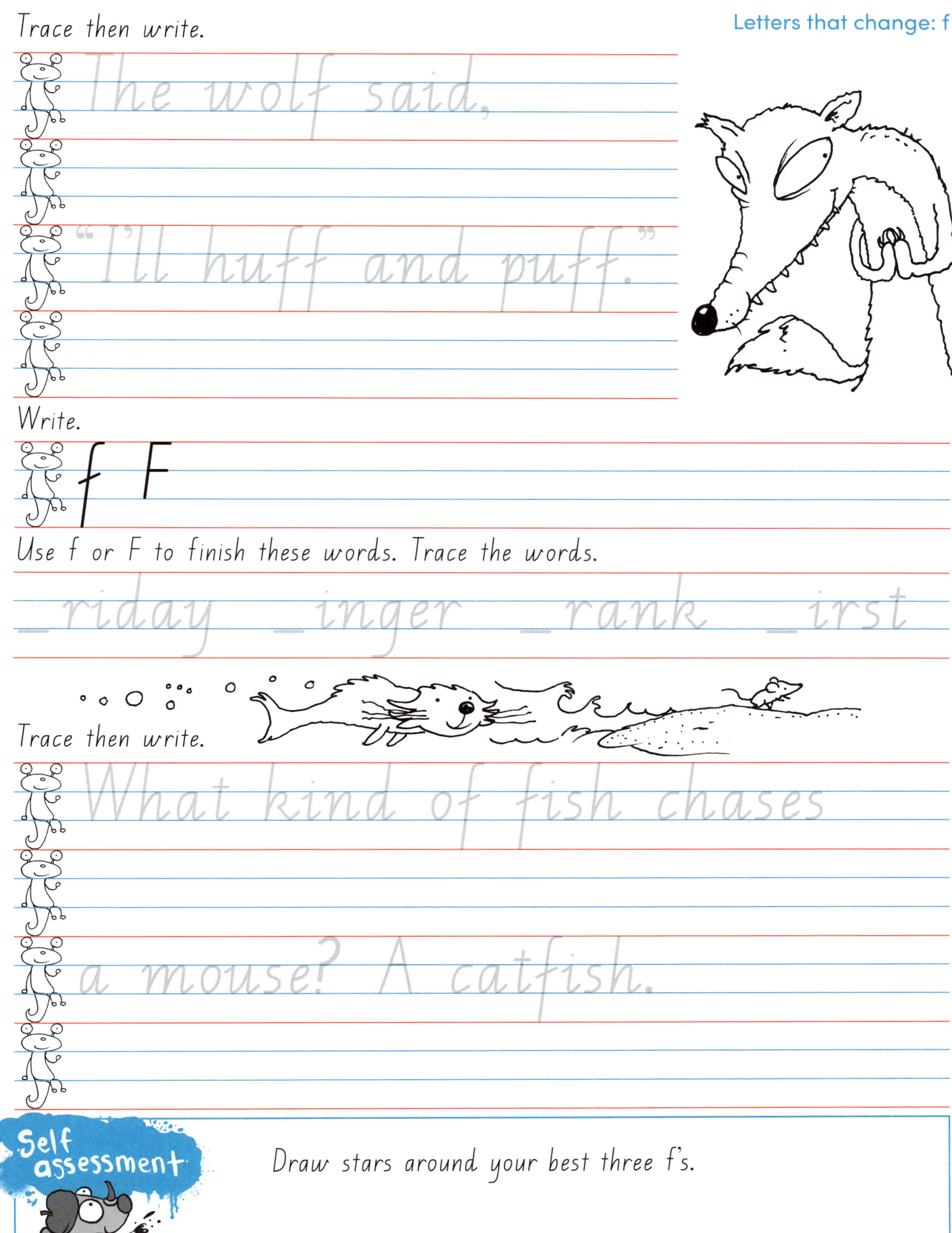

Trace then write.

The wolf said,

"I'll huff and puff."

Write.

f F

Use f or F to finish these words. Trace the words.

_riday _inger _rank _irst

Trace then write.

What kind of fish chases

a mouse? A catfish.

Self assessment

Draw stars around your best three f's.

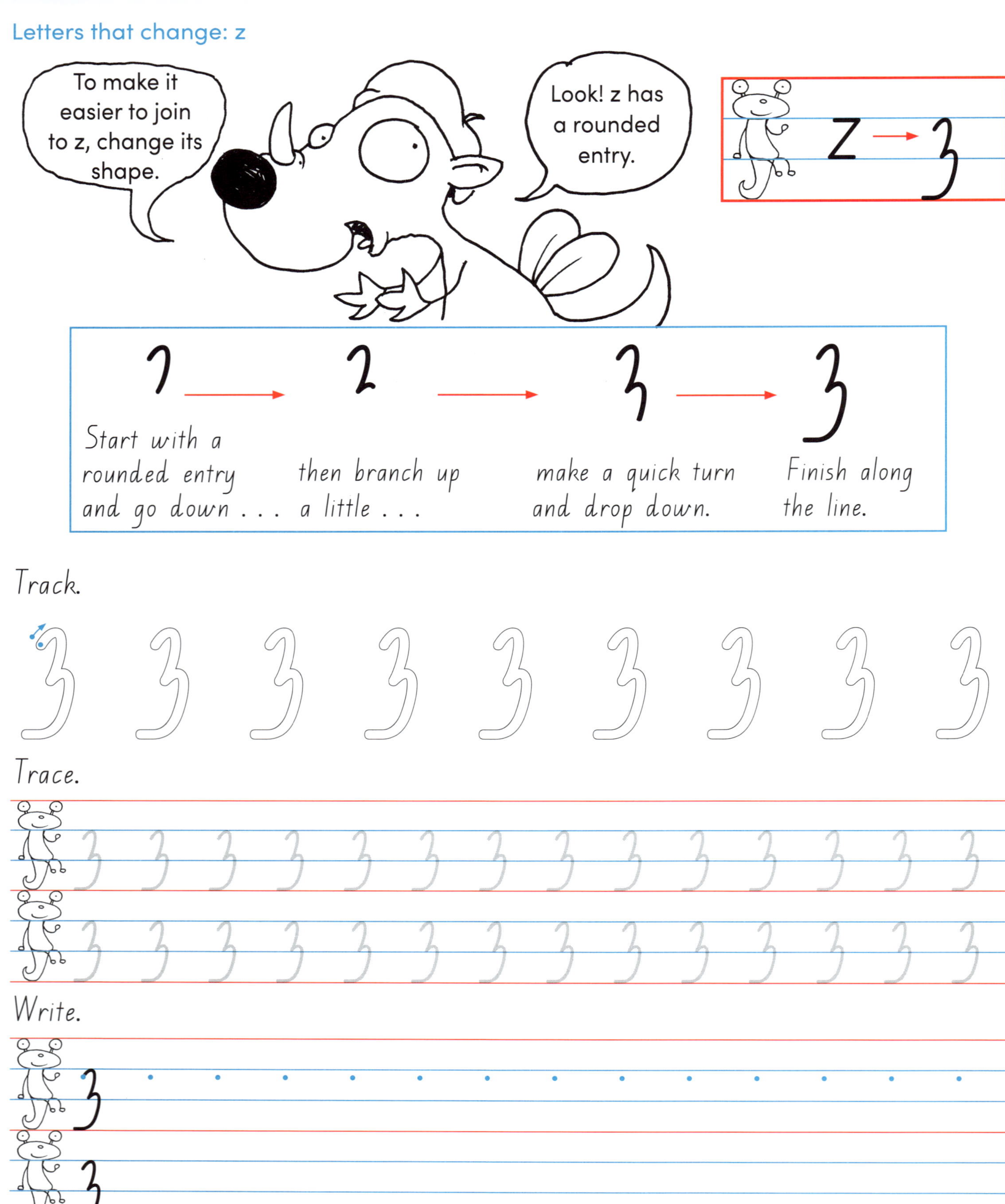

Handwriting: letters that change (z).
Grammar: question; question word (how); doing verb (zoom); prepositional phrases (to school, In a buzz).
Punctuation: upper-case (capital) letter to start a sentence; question mark.
Spelling and vocabulary: rhyme (sizzle/grizzle); vowel digraph 'oo' (school, zoom).
Literary elements: onomatopoeia (sizzle, fizz, zap, zing, zip); riddle; word play (buzz/bus).

Trace then write.

fizz fizzy fizzle sizzle dazzle

zap zing zip grizzle nuzzle zoo

Write.

z Z

Trace then write.

How does a bee get to

school? In a buzz.

Draw stars around your best three z's.

Letters that don't change: b, g, o, q, s

b g o q s

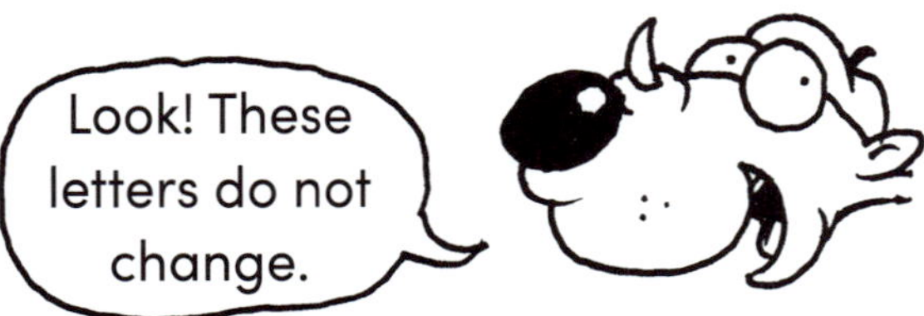

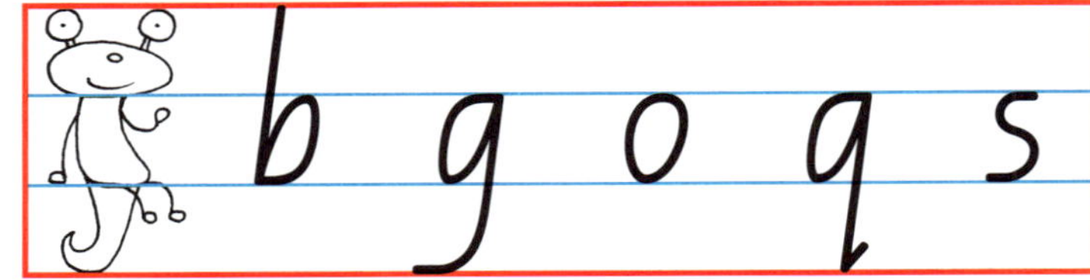

Trace. Make any changes you need to and add entries and exits. Remember the letters that do not change.

a b c d e f g h i

j k l m n o p q r

s t u v w x y z

Trace then write.

quiz quit

quite quiet

question quote

quick quack

Trace.

Be happy with what you've got.

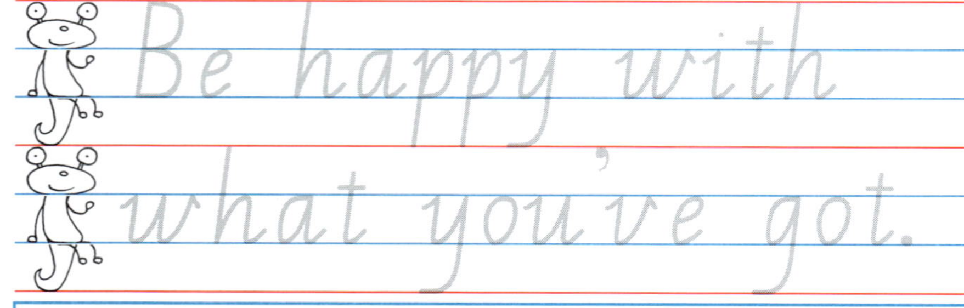

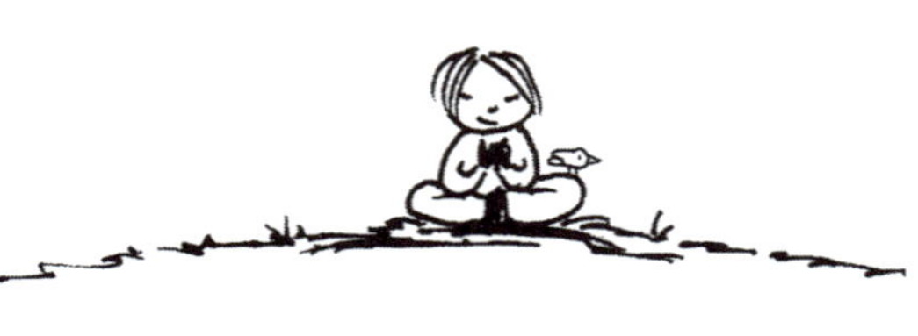

Handwriting: letters that don't change (b, g, o, q, s). (Now do Progressive Assessment 5, page 64.)
Grammar: statement; question; question word (what); adjectives (shabby, glossy); contraction (you've); prepositional phrase (to the moo-vies).
Punctuation: upper-case (capital) letter to start a sentence; question mark; full stop.
Spelling and vocabulary: 'qu' words; words ending in 'y'; double letter words.
Literary elements: moral (a bird in the hand is worth two in the bush, from various origins including Aesop's fable 'The Hawk and the Nightingale'); riddle; word play (moo-vies/movies).

Trace then write the matching lower-case letters. Letters that don't change: b, g, o, q, s

B G O Q S

Trace then write.

shaggy baggy

shabby flabby

bossy glossy

wobbly bobbly

Trace then write.

What does the cow like to

do on her day off? She goes

to the moo-vies.

Self assessment

Rate your writing: needs improvement ☐

improving consistently ☐

consistently good. ☐

Diagonal joins to rounded entries

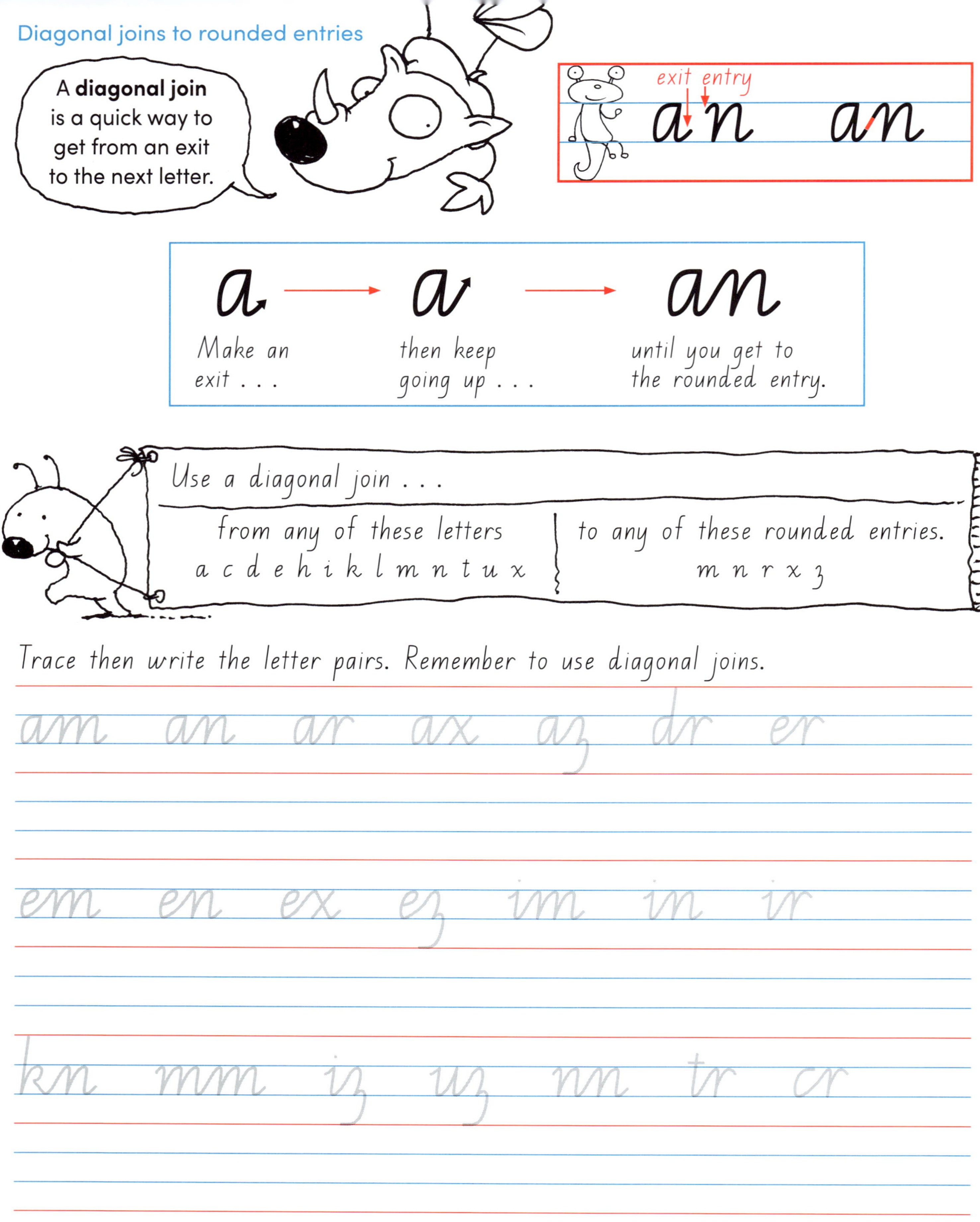

Trace then write the letter pairs. Remember to use diagonal joins.

am an ar ax az dr er

em en ex ez im in ir

kn mm iz uz nn tr cr

Handwriting: diagonal joins.
Spelling and vocabulary: common letter pairs.

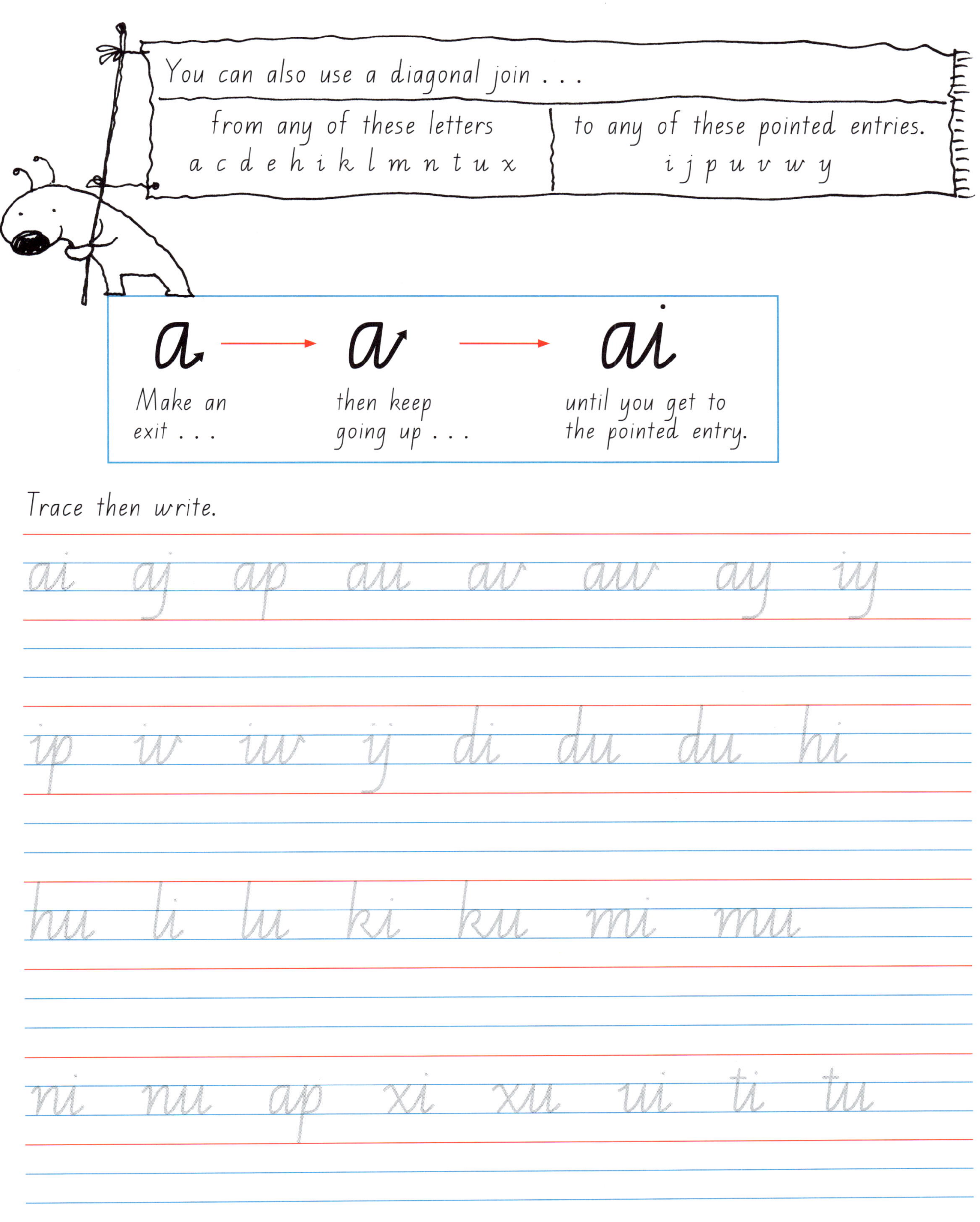
You can also use a diagonal join . . .
from any of these letters
a c d e h i k l m n t u x
to any of these pointed entries.
i j p u v w y
a
Make an exit . . .
a
then keep going up . . .
ai
until you get to the pointed entry.
Trace then write.
ai aj ap au av aw ay iy
ip iv iw ij di du du hi
hu li lu ki ku mi mu
ni nu ap xi xu ui ti tu

You can also use a diagonal join . . .

from any of these letters	to any of these tall letters.
a c d e h i k l m n t u x	b h k l t

a → al → al

Make an exit . . . then keep going up all the way . . . then retrace to make the next letter.

Trace then write.

ah al ak at dh dk dl dt

lk ik il it th el et eh ek

Trace then write.

If you can't beat

them, join them.

Boing

Self assessment

My diagonal joins are smooth:

sometimes ☐ often ☐ always ☐.

Some letters join by lifting your pencil and dropping the letter onto an exit.

Use exits from any of these letters	to drop on any of these letters.
a c d e h i k l m n t u x	a c d g q

Trace then write.

ac ad ag aq ca cc cd

da dg ea ec ed eg eq

ha ia ic id ig iq ka

la ld ac ad ag ca da

Handwriting: dropping on letters. (over page)
Grammar: question; question word (what); personal pronouns (you, them); verb group (contraction: can't); subordinating conjunction (If): dependent and independent clause.
Punctuation: upper-case (capital) letter to start a sentence; question mark.
Literary elements: riddle.

Remember to make sure your writing hand and arm can move freely.

Trace then write.

la ld ma na ta uc ud ug xa

lad glad mad sag rag tag

had day bed red dad

Trace then write.

What pie can fly?

A magpie.

Self assessment

My joins are smooth when I drop on letters:

sometimes ☐ often ☐ always ☐.

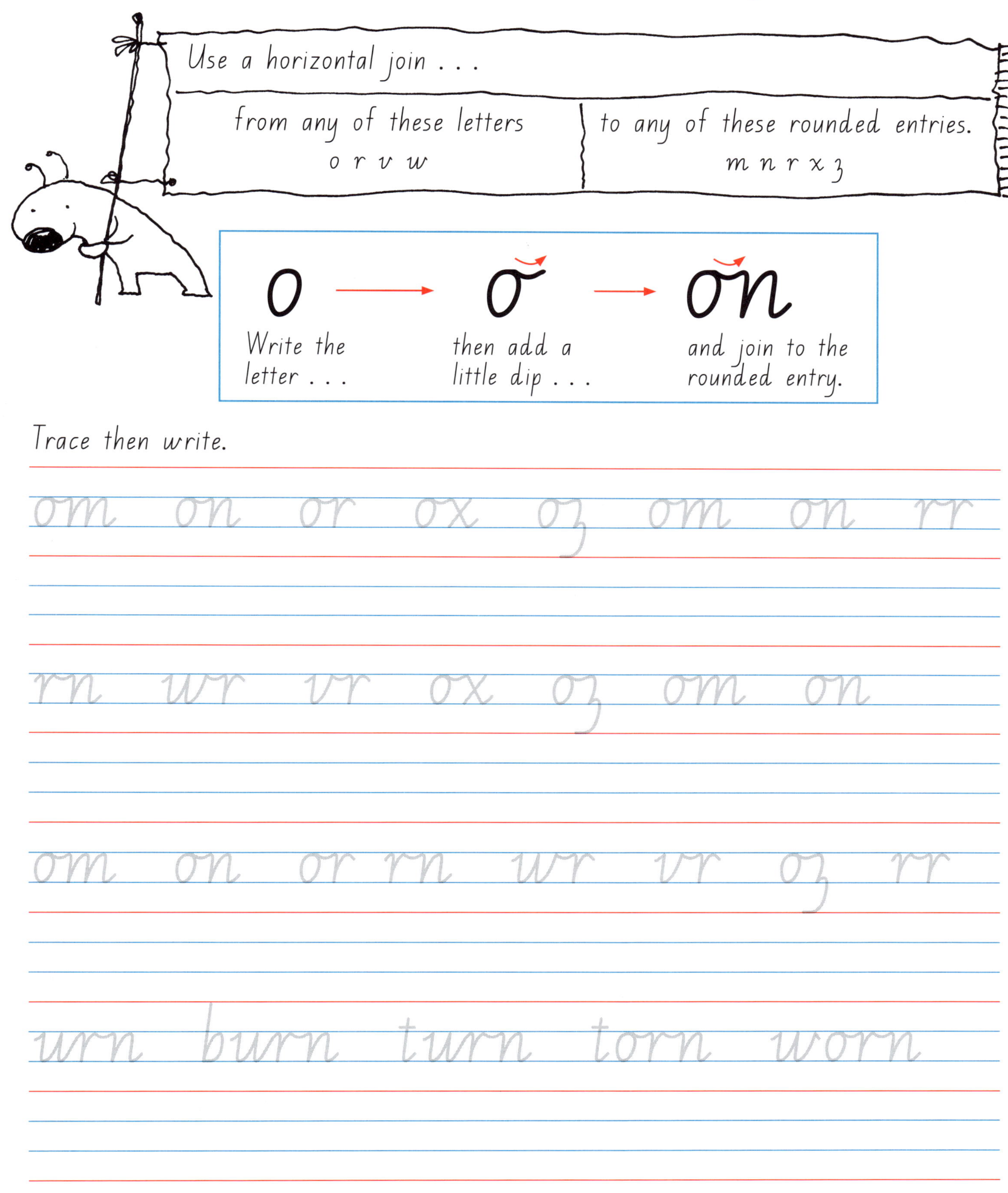

Handwriting: horizontal joins to rounded entries.
Spelling and vocabulary: rhyme (urn/burn, torn/worn).

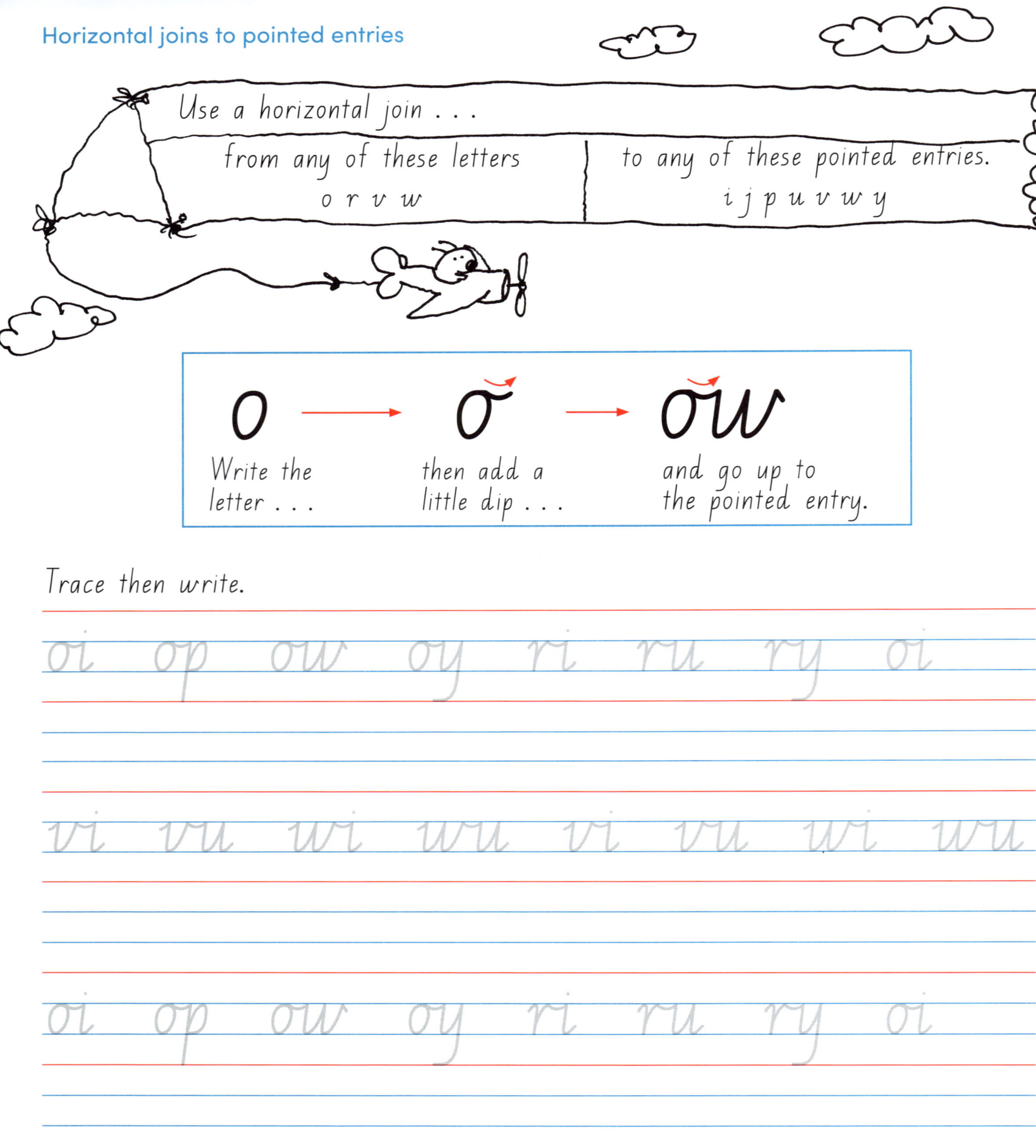

Trace then write.

oi op ow oy ri ru ry oi

vi vu wi wu vi vu wi wu

oi op ow oy ri ru ry oi

vi vu wi wu vi vu wi wu

You need a horizontal join . . .

from any of these letters	to sweep up to these tall letters.
o r v w	b h k l t

Trace then write.

ob oh ok ol ot ob oh ol

rk rb rk rb rk rb rk rb

Trace then write.

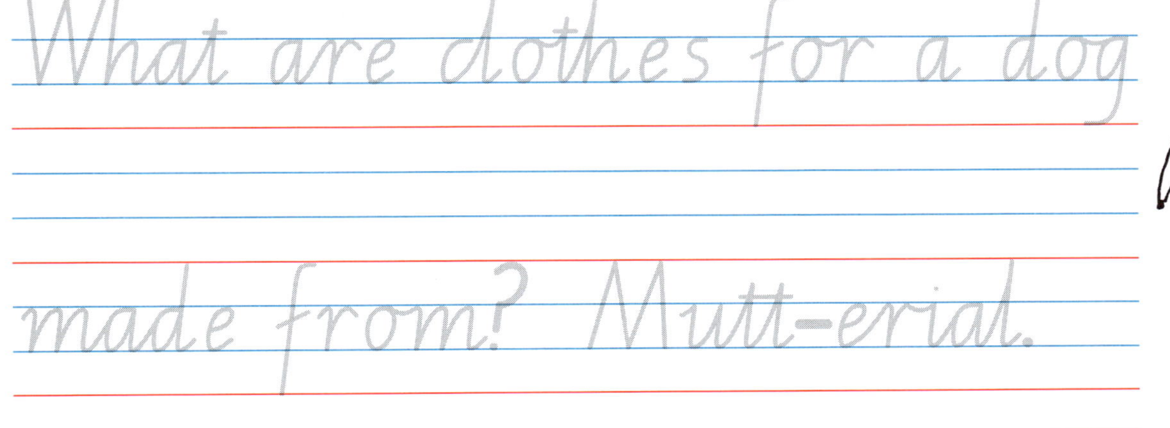

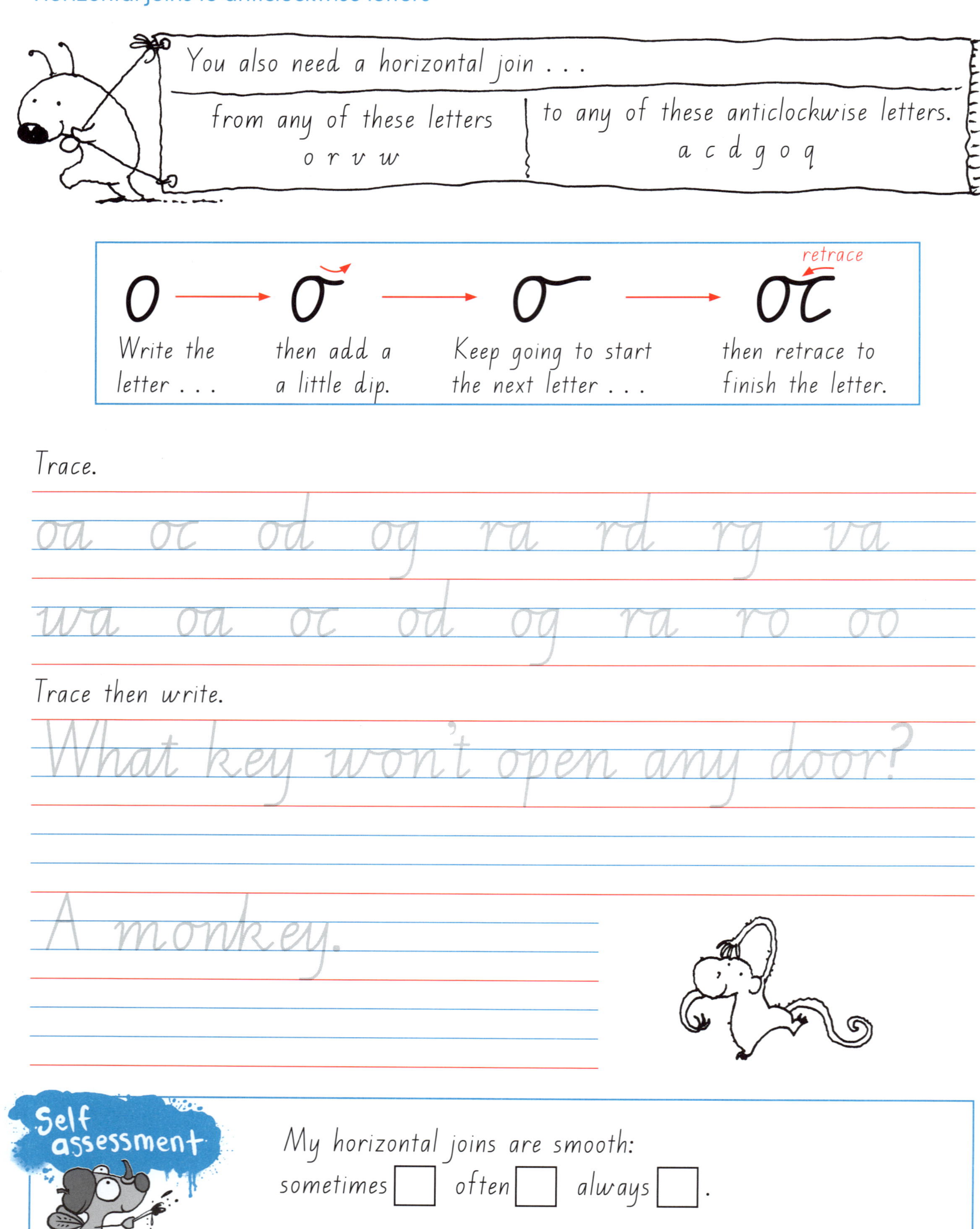

You also need a horizontal join . . .

from any of these letters	to any of these anticlockwise letters.
o r v w	a c d g o q

Trace.

oa oc od og ra rd rg va

wa oa oc od og ra ro oo

Trace then write.

What key won't open any door?

A monkey.

Self assessment

My horizontal joins are smooth:

sometimes ☐ often ☐ always ☐.

Trace then write.

Where did Tyrannosaurus

rex live?

Anywhere it wanted to.

See you later alligator.

In a while crocodile.

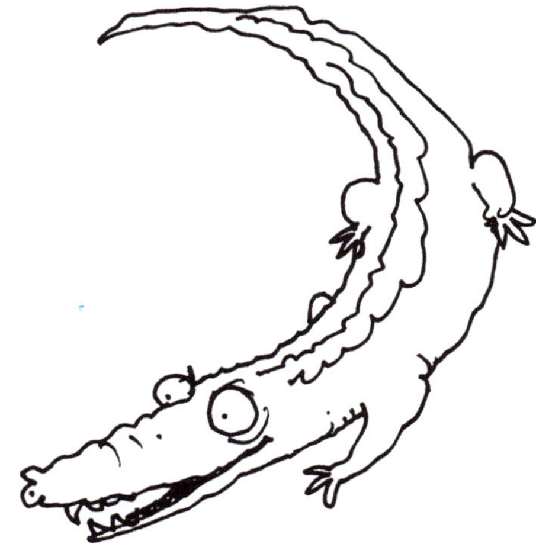

Handwriting: practising joins. (Now do Progressive Assessment 6, page 64.)
Punctuation: upper-case (capital) letter to start a sentence; question mark; full stop.
Grammar: question; question word (where); statement; proper noun (Tyrannosaurus); prepositional phrase (in a while); personal pronouns (it, you); noun group (any door); noun – pronoun reference (Tyrannosaurus Rex–it).
Spelling and vocabulary: compound word (anywhere); digraph 'wh' (where, while); rhyme (later/alligator, while/crocodile).
Literary elements: joke; colloquialisms/sayings and expressions.

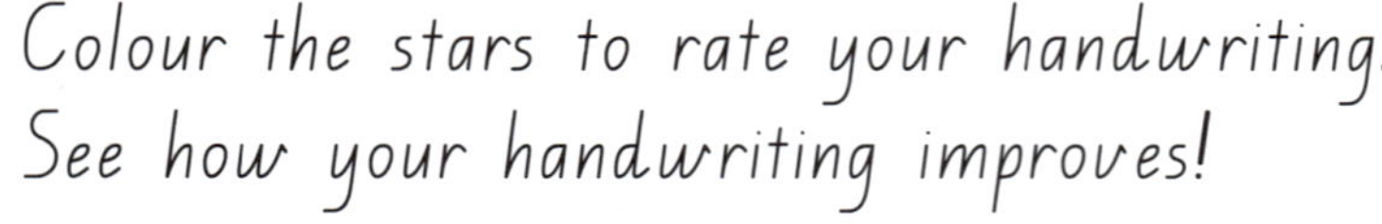

Colour the stars to rate your handwriting.
See how your handwriting improves!

Assessment 1 Date ____________

The quick brown fox jumps over
the lazy dog.

Rating ☆ ☆ ☆ ☆ ☆

Assessment 2 Date ____________

The quick brown fox jumps over
the lazy dog.

Rating ☆ ☆ ☆ ☆ ☆

Assessment 3 Date ______________________

The quick brown fox jumps over
the lazy dog.

Rating ☆ ☆ ☆ ☆ ☆

Assessment 4 Date ______________________

The quick brown fox jumps over
the lazy dog.

Rating ☆ ☆ ☆ ☆ ☆

Progressive assessments continued

Assessment 5 Date ____________

The quick brown fox jumps over
the lazy dog.

Rating ☆ ☆ ☆ ☆ ☆

Assessment 6 Date ____________

The quick brown fox jumps over
the lazy dog.

Rating ☆ ☆ ☆ ☆ ☆